Ange

By United Library

https://campsite.bio/unitedlibrary

Table of Contents

Disclaimer

This biography book is a work of nonfiction based on the public life of a famous person. The author has used publicly available information to create this work. While the author has thoroughly researched the subject and attempted to depict it accurately, it is not meant to be an exhaustive study of the subject. The views expressed in this book are those of the author alone and do not necessarily reflect those of any organization associated with the subject. This book should not be taken as an endorsement, legal advice, or any other form of professional advice. This book was written for entertainment purposes only.

Introduction

Embark on an intimate exploration of the life and legacy of Angelina Jolie, the iconic American actress, filmmaker and humanitarian. Born Angelina Jolie Voight on June 4, 1975, Jolie's journey through the realms of Hollywood has been nothing short of extraordinary. Winner of an Oscar and three Golden Globes, she has consistently been recognized as Hollywood's highest paid actress.

From her early days alongside her father, Jon Voight, in "Lookin' to Get Out" (1982), to her leading role in the low-budget production "Cyborg 2" (1993), Jolie's cinematic evolution is captivating. Her rise continued with leading roles in "Hackers" (1995), the biographical television films "George Wallace" (1997) and "Gia" (1998), and her Oscar-winning performance in "Girl, Interrupted" (1999). The action film "Lara Croft: Tomb Raider" (2001) firmly established her as a force in cinema, followed by hits such as "Mr. and Mrs. Smith" (2005), "Wanted" (2008) and "Salt" (2010).

Beyond the screen, Jolie's forays into directing, including "In the Land of Blood and Honey" (2011) and "Invincible" (2014), reveal her skill behind the camera. Known for her humanitarian efforts, Jolie's advocacy on behalf of refugees as Special Envoy of the United Nations High

Commissioner for Refugees has earned her numerous accolades, including the Jean Hersholt Humanitarian Award.

This book offers an in-depth look at her multifaceted career, her impactful humanitarian work and her engaging personal journey, making it a must-read for fans and those intrigued by the woman behind the Hollywood spotlight.

Angelina Jolie

Angelina Jolie Voight (Los Angeles, June 4, 1975) is an American actress, filmmaker and humanitarian activist. She made her film debut alongside her father, Jon Voight, in *Lookin' to Get Out* (1982); however, her career began in earnest a decade later, when she appeared in the low-budget film *Cyborg 2* (1993), followed by her first leading role in a major production in *Hackers* (1995). She was later cast in the biographical telefilms *George Wallace* (1997), for which she won her first Golden Globe Award for Best Supporting Actress in a Television Movie and received a Primetime Emmy Award nomination for Best Supporting Actress in a Miniseries or Television Movie, and *Gia* (1998), winning the Golden Globe again, only this time in the category of Best Actress in a Miniseries or Television Movie. In 1999, she received praise from specialized critics for her performance as Lisa Rowe in the film *Girl, Interrupted,* for which she won the Oscar for Best Supporting Actress.

Jolie gained international recognition in 2001 for playing the video game heroine Lara Croft in *Tomb Raider*, thus establishing herself among Hollywood's leading actresses. She continued her career as an "action star" in *Mr. & Mrs. Smith* (2005), *Wanted* (2008), *Salt* and *The Tourist* (both 2010). The actress was praised by critics for her performances in the dramas *A Mighty Heart* (2007) and *Changeling* (2008), which earned her her second Oscar nomination in the Best Actress category. Her biggest commercial success came with the fantasy film *Maleficent* (2014). From the 2010s, she expanded her career into directing, screenwriting and producing, directing the war dramas *In the Land of Blood and Honey* (2011) and *Unbroken* (2014). As of April 2019, she was one of the highest-grossing actresses of all time in North America, as well as in the top 110 overall, with her films making over 2.17 billion dollars.

In addition to her film work, Angelina Jolie is known for her humanitarian efforts, for which she has received a Jean Hersholt Humanitarian Award and the honorary title of Dame of the Order of St. Michael and St. George (DCMG), among other distinctions. She promotes various causes, including environmental conservation, education and women's rights, and is best known for her advocacy on behalf of refugees, having been appointed Special Envoy for the United Nations High Commissioner for Refugees (UNHCR).

As a public figure, Jolie is cited as one of the most influential and powerful people in the American entertainment industry, as well as the most beautiful woman in the world, by various media, which consider her a sex symbol. In 2006, *People* magazine named her the Most Beautiful Person in the World, while *Empire* and *Esquire named* her the Sexiest Movie Star Ever. She was named the world's most powerful celebrity by *Forbes* in 2009, as well as the most powerful actress from 2006 to 2008 and from 2011 to 2013. In 2009, 2011 and 2013, she was the highest paid actress in Hollywood. Her personal life is the subject of constant media attention. She divorced actors Jonny Lee Miller, Billy Bob Thornton and Brad Pitt, with whom she had six children, three of whom were adopted.

Early years and adolescence

Angelina Jolie Voight was born in Los Angeles, California. She is the daughter of actors Jon Voight and Marcheline Bertrand, niece of Chip Taylor, sister of James Haven Voight and goddaughter of Jacqueline Bisset and Maximilian Schell. On her father's side, she is of Slovak and German descent; on the other hand, her mother had French, Dutch and German ancestry. Like her mother, Jolie claimed to be part Iroquois, as well as having a remote indigenous Huronian ancestor, born in 1649.

After her parents separated in 1976, Jolie and her brother moved in with their mother, who had abandoned her artistic ambitions to concentrate on raising her children. As a child, Jolie often watched movies with her mother, and it was this, rather than her father's successful career, that sparked her interest in acting; although, at the age of five, she had taken part in the movie *Lookin' to Get Out* (1982), alongside Voight. At the age of six, Bertrand and her partner, filmmaker Bill Day, moved with their family to Palisades, New York; they returned to Los Angeles five years later. Then Jolie decided she wanted to act and enrolled at the Lee Strasberg Theatre Institute in Los

Angeles, where she studied for two years and, during that time, appeared in several theater productions; she also attended Beverly Hills High School, where she felt isolated from the children of wealthier families in the area, since her mother had a more modest income. She was teased by other students, who made fun of her for being extremely thin and for wearing glasses and braces.

At her mother's insistence, she considered a career in modeling; however, her first attempts at the profession proved unsuccessful. Jolie abandoned her acting classes and became interested in the funeral director's profession, taking correspondence courses on how to prepare bodies for funerals. Subsequently, she transferred to Moreno High School, an alternative school, where she became a "weird *punk*," dyed her hair purple, wore black clothes and participated in circle jerks with her then-boyfriend, with whom she lived together and experimented with sadomasochism. At sixteen, after the relationship ended, Jolie graduated from school and rented her own apartment, before returning to her theater studies. In 2004, in reference to this period, she remarked: "I'm still deep down - and always will be - just a *punk* girl with tattoos."

While still in her teens, Jolie found it difficult to connect emotionally with other people and, as a result, self-harmed, an act about which she commented: "For some reason, the ritual of cutting myself and feeling the pain, feeling some kind of release, was somehow therapeutic for me." She also struggled with insomnia and an eating disorder, and began experimenting with drugs; by the age of twenty, she had used "almost every drug possible," particularly heroin. She also suffered episodes of depression and planned to commit suicide twice, at nineteen and again at twenty-two, at which age she tried to hire a hitman to kill her. At the age of 24, she had a nervous breakdown; as a result, she was hospitalized for 72 hours in the psychiatric ward of the UCLA Medical Center. Two years later, after adopting her first son, she found stability in her life, and said: "I knew that once I committed myself to Maddox [her son], I would never be self-destructive again."

Jon Voight abandoned the family when Jolie was less than a year old, eventually culminating in a dysfunctional relationship between them. From then on, their moments together were rare and usually only when they appeared in public. However, they eventually reconciled when they acted together in *Lara Croft: Tomb Raider* (2001) but, nevertheless, their relationship deteriorated again. The actress then decided to legally remove the surname "Voight" to just her middle name, which she had been using for some time as a stage name; the name change was granted on September 12, 2002. Jon then made their disagreement public during an appearance on *Access*

Hollywood, in which he claimed that his daughter had "serious mental problems." At this point, Marcheline Bertrand and James Haven also broke off contact with Jon, going six and a half years without establishing contact; however, they began to rebuild their relationship close to Bertrand's death on January 27, 2007, from ovarian cancer. Three years later, Voight's reconciliation with Jolie became public.

Careers

1991-1997: First works

Jolie committed to acting professionally at the age of sixteen; however, she initially found it difficult to pass casting tests, as casting producers noted that her demeanor was "too dark." She appeared in five of her brother's student films, made while they were attending the USC School of Cinema-Television, as well as in several music videos, namely "Stand by My Woman" (1991), by Lenny Kravitz; "Alta Marea", by Antonello Venditti (1991); "It's About Time" (1993), by The Lemonheads; and "Rock and Roll Dreams Come Through" (1993), by Meat Loaf.

She began her professional film career in 1993, when she played her first leading role in the science fiction sequel *Cyborg 2*, as an "almost human" robot designed for corporate espionage and assassination. She was so disappointed with the movie that she didn't audition again for a year. After a supporting role in *Without Evidence* (1995), she starred in the film *Hackers* (1995). Janet Maslin of the *New York Times* noted that the actress stood out from her cast mates. The production failed to make a profit at the box office, but developed a *cult* following after its release on DVD. After starring in *Love Is All There Is* (1996), a modern adaptation of Romeo and

Juliet, the actress appeared in the film *Mojave Moon* (1996); about her performance in this, *The Hollywood Reporter* wrote: "Jolie, an actress the camera really adores, reveals a comic talent and the kind of passionate sexuality that makes her entirely believable and Danny Aiello's character would drop everything just for the chance to be with her."

In 1997, Jolie starred in the film *Playing God,* set in the criminal underworld of Los Angeles, with David Duchovny. The production was not well received by critics; Roger Ebert of the *Chicago Sun-Times* noted that the actress "finds a certain enthusiasm in a type of role that is usually tough and aggressive, she seems too cool to be [a mobster's] girlfriend, and maybe she is." She also played a *stripper* who abandons her performance to tour New York City in the music video for "Anybody Seen My Baby?" by The Rolling Stones.

1998-2000: Breakthrough

Her career prospects began to improve after the actress won a Golden Globe for her performance as Cornelia in the 1997 George Wallace biopic, in which she was considered "a standout in the making" by *The Philadelphia Inquirer*. The film was also very well received by critics and won, among other awards, the Golden Globe for Best Miniseries or Television Movie. She was also nominated for an Emmy for Best Supporting Actress in a Miniseries or Telefilm.

Her first major breakthrough came when she played supermodel Gia Carangi in the telefilm *Gia* (1998), which chronicles the destruction of Carangi's life and career as a result of her heroin addiction, her decline and death from AIDS in the mid-1980s. Vanessa Vance of Reel.com noted retrospectively: "Jolie won wide acclaim for her role as Gia, and it's easy to see why. She is fierce in her performance - filling it with nerves, charm and desperation - and her role in this movie is possibly the most beautiful 'disaster' [about a person's life] ever filmed." For the second year running, the actress won a Golden Globe, this time for Best Actress in a Miniseries or Telefilm, and her first Screen Actors Guild Award, and was nominated for an Emmy in the same category.

Following Lee Strasberg's The Method, Jolie preferred to stay in character even after shooting her scenes in many of her early films, and as a result gained a reputation for being difficult to deal with. After filming of *Gia* finished, she briefly gave up acting because she felt she had "nothing more to give." She separated from her husband Jonny Lee Miller and moved to New York, where she took night classes in directing and screenwriting at New York University. Encouraged by her Golden Globe win for *George Wallace* and the positive critical reception of *Gia, she* resumed her career. After appearing in the film *Hell's Kitchen* (1998), she acted in *Playing by Heart* (1998), which received predominantly positive reviews and for which she was particularly praised, winning the Breakthrough Actress award from the National Board of Review.

In 1999, she starred in the dramatic comedy *Pushing Tin,* alongside Cate Blanchett, Billy Bob Thornton and John Cusack, which received a mixed reception from critics, and her character - Thornton's seductive wife - was particularly criticized. Jolie co-starred with Denzel Washington in *The Bone Collector* (1999), playing a policewoman who reluctantly helps a quadriplegic detective track down a serial killer. The film grossed 151.5 million dollars worldwide, but received poor critical reviews. Terry Lawson, of the *Detroit Free Press,* concluded: "Jolie, while always pleasant to look at, was woefully miscast."; Pablo Villaça added: "With better material at hand, Jolie would certainly have stood out."

The actress then played Lisa Rowe, a sociopathic patient, in *Girl, Interrupted* (1999), an adaptation of Susanna Kaysen's book of the same name. Although the film was expected to mark a major career comeback for Winona Ryder, who played the main character, it was Jolie who received great acclaim from film critics and took a big step forward in the Hollywood industry. For *Variety*, Emanuel

Levy observed: "Jolie is excellent as the flamboyant, irresponsible girl." In his review for *The New York Times*, Stephen Holden wrote that "Jolie's fierce, thrilling performance captures the frightening allure of this adventurous, brutal movie." Critic Roger Ebert praised her performance, saying: "The actress is emerging as one of the great wild spirits of movies today, a loose cannon who somehow has deadly aim." As a result, she won her third Golden Globe, her second Screen Actors Guild and her first Critics Choice and Oscar, all in the category of Best Supporting Actress, as well as being awarded the trophy for Actress of the Year by the Hollywood Film Festival and Best Supporting Actress by the National Association of Theater Owners.

"Her performances in *Girl, Interrupted* and especially *Gia* may be the most powerful [by an American actor] of the last twenty years. It's impossible to imagine any other actress in these roles; at her best, Jolie makes almost every other actress of her generation look timid."

- Allen Barra, *Salon.com* critic, praising Jolie's performances

In 2000, she appeared in *Gone in 60 Seconds,* which became her highest-grossing film to date, earning 237.2 million dollars internationally, and in which she had a small role as a mechanic and ex-girlfriend of a car thief played by Nicolas Cage. Regarding the actress's participation, Stephen Hunter, for the *Washington Post,* wrote: "all she does in this movie is stand and move those plump, pulsating lips that nestle so provocatively in her teeth."

2001-2004: International recognition

Despite being highly praised for her acting skills, Jolie had not found films that appealed to a wide audience; however, she achieved international recognition when she landed the role of Lara Croft in *Tomb Raider* (2001). In this adaptation of the popular video game series, the actress was required to learn an English accent and undergo extensive martial arts training. Her casting for the role generated controversy because, according to those who were against it, she didn't have the right physique, she was an American playing an originally British character, she had tattoos and other factors related to her personal life which, theoretically, made her incompatible for the role. In view of this, the film's director, Simon West, defended her from the moment the first media fuss was made, gradually making it dissipate. During filming, the actress dispensed with stunt doubles for the action scenes, and this led to her being injured.

Although the movie generated negative reviews, she was generally praised for her mainly physical performance. According to the *Rotten Tomatoes* critical consensus, "Angelina Jolie is perfect for the role of Lara Croft, but

[even] she can't save the movie from a nonsensical plot and action sequences that lack emotional impact"; Sebastian Zavala agreed, saying that the actress's presence on camera "is so magnetic." John Anderson, from *Newsday,* commented: "Jolie makes the title character a virtual icon of female competence and coolness." Marcelo Forlani, in his review for *Omelete,* considered her perfect for the role. The film was an international box office success, earning 274.7 million dollars worldwide, and became the film starring a woman with the best debut, 48 million dollars in three days; after three weeks, it surpassed the 100 million barrier. The film earned Jolie an international reputation as an "action star," and *Forbes* film critic Scott Mendelson published an article whose headline refers to the actress as the "first female movie star in the blockbuster action genre."

Jolie starred as the mail-order bride of Antonio Banderas' character in *Original Sin* (2001). *New York Times* critic Elvis Mitchell questioned her decision to pursue a career with "*soft-core* nonsense." The romantic comedy *Life or Something Like It* (2002), was equally unsuccessful. By 2002, she had established herself among the highest paid actresses in Hollywood, earning between ten and fifteen million dollars per film.

Jolie reprised her role as Lara Croft in *Tomb Raider - The Cradle of Life* (2003), which was not as lucrative as the original, earning 156.5 million dollars at the international box office; in addition, she starred in the music video for Korn's "Did My Time", used to promote the sequel. Her next film was *Beyond Borders* (2003), in which she played a socialite who has a relationship with a humanitarian worker played by Clive Owen. Although it didn't do well at the box office, the film was the first of several projects that made Jolie join humanitarian causes. Kenneth Turan of the *Los Angeles Times* recognized the actress's ability to "bring emotion and credibility to the role."

In 2004, four films were released with Jolie. She first starred in the thriller *Taking Lives* as an FBI profiler called in to help the Montreal police arrest a serial killer. The film received mixed reviews; Kirk Honeycutt, for *The Hollywood Reporter,* concluded: "Jolie plays a role that [she] definitely feels like something she's done before, but adds an unmistakable dash of excitement and glamor." She subsequently made a brief appearance in *Sky Captain and the World of Tomorrow*, a science fiction adventure that was filmed entirely with the actors in front of *chroma key,* and voiced her first children's movie, the animated *Shark Tale*. Her supporting role as Queen Olympia of Epirus in *Alexander*, about the life of Alexander the Great, was met with a mixed reception, particularly in relation to her Slavic accent. Commercially, the film flopped in North America, causing director Oliver Stone to blame disapproval of the portrayal of

Alexander's bisexuality, but it managed to gross 167.3 million dollars internationally.

2005-2010: Commercial and critical success

In 2005, Jolie was cast in the action comedy *Mr. & Mrs. Smith*, in which she starred alongside Brad Pitt as a couple who discover that they are both secret assassins. The film received mixed reviews, but was generally praised for the chemistry between the lead actors, and became a box office success. Roger Ebert said that "what makes the movie work is that Pitt and Jolie have fun together on screen and are able to find a rhythm that allows them to be understated and entertaining, even during the most alarming developments." Manohla Dargis of *The New York Times* wrote: "This is Brad and Angelina's *show and not much else. That's too bad, because both actors are capable of more." With a worldwide take of 478.2 million dollars, *Mr. & Mrs. Smith* went on to become the seventh highest grossing film of the year and remained Jolie's most lucrative action film until the following decade.

After a supporting role as the neglected wife of a CIA officer in *The Good Shepherd* (2006), Jolie starred as Mariane Pearl in the documentary drama *A Mighty Heart* (2007). Based on the book of the same name, the film chronicles the kidnapping and murder of her husband, *Wall Street Journal* reporter Daniel Pearl, in Pakistan. Although Pearl personally chose Jolie for the role, racial criticism and accusations of *blackface* arose. The actress's performance was widely praised, including by *The Hollywood Reporter*, with analyst Ray Bennett describing it as "well-measured and moving," and played "with respect." She received nominations for the Golden Globe for Best Actress in a Motion Picture, Critics' Choice Movie, Independent Spirit, Satellite and Screen Actors Guild Award for Best Actress, and also directed the documentary *A Place in Time*. Also in 2007, she played Grendel's mother in the epic *Beowulf*, created through motion capture. The film was critically and commercially well received, grossing 196.4 million dollars worldwide."

In 2008, Jolie was the highest paid actress in Hollywood, earning between fifteen and twenty million dollars per film. While other actresses were forced to take pay cuts in previous years, the box office success Jolie brought to the films she starred in allowed her to earn as much as twenty million, plus a percentage. She acted alongside James McAvoy and Morgan Freeman in the action film *Wanted* (2008), which grossed 341.4 million dollars worldwide. The film received predominantly favorable reviews. Writing for *The New York Times*, Manohla Dargis noted that "Jolie was perfectly cast as a super-scary, seemingly amoral killer." Pablo Villaça, from *Cinema em Cena, wrote* that "she goes through the movie on autopilot, relying on her beauty to turn Fox [her character] into a relevant figure - and she succeeds (watch, for example, the very sensual way she lies on a moving train and you'll see an actress fully aware of the power of her body over the viewer)." *Time ranked* her fifth among the ten best performances of the year.

Jolie took on the lead role in Clint Eastwood's drama *Changeling* (2008). Based on the Wineville Crimes, which took place in Los Angeles in 1928, the film focuses on Christine Collins, a woman who rediscovers a boy who was supposed to be her missing son, and soon realizes that he is not actually her son. The actress received acclaim from the specialized critics; Amir Labaki, in his review written for *Folha de S.Paulo*, described this as "her best role, [...] Jolie has never been better," and added: "Fury and fragility, intelligence and emotion, temper and skepticism blend in a performance that is bigger than awards, bigger than films, bigger than life." Pablo Villaça praised the actress, saying that she "sensitively portrays the pain of a mother facing the worst tragedy imaginable for those who have children. In fact, Jolie's performance is so effective that, even though the movie doesn't try to explain the woman's actions, we understand why she agrees to take a strange child home." Kirk Honeycutt of *The Hollywood Reporter* noted that "she delivers a powerful emotional display as a tenacious woman who gathers strength over the forces that oppose her, and reminds us that there's nothing quite so fierce as a mother protecting her child." Jolie has received BAFTA,

Critics' Choice Movie, Empire, Golden Globe, Screen Actors Guild and Academy Award nominations for Best Actress and has won the Satellite and Saturn awards in the same category. She also lent her voice to the animation *Kung Fu Panda* (2008), her first major role in a children's franchise, later reprising her role in the sequels *Kung Fu Panda 2 (*2011) and *Kung Fu Panda 3* (2016).

After her mother's death in 2007, Jolie began appearing in fewer films, explaining that her motivation to be an actress stemmed from her mother's acting ambitions. Her first film in two years was the spy thriller *Salt* (2010), in which she starred as a CIA agent who is pursued after being accused of being a KGB sleeper agent. Originally written for a male character, with Tom Cruise tipped to star, Agent Salt underwent a gender change after a Columbia Pictures executive suggested Jolie for the role. With revenues of 293.5 million dollars, it became an international success. The film received generally positive reviews, with Jolie's performance in particular winning praise. Critic William Thomas of *Empire* magazine commented: "When it comes to selling incredible, crazy, death-defying fantasies, Jolie has few competitors in the action business."

She starred alongside Johnny Depp in the action film *The Tourist* (2010), which received less than favorable reviews from critics, although Roger Ebert defended Jolie's performance, stating that she "does her most terrifying" and "plays her femme fatale with intensity and a ravishing sexuality." Despite a slow start at the American box office, the film grossed 278.3 million dollars worldwide, increasing Jolie's appeal to international audiences. She received a Golden Globe nomination for her performance.

Also in 2010, speculation arose that she would play Marilyn Monroe in the movie *The life and opinions of Maf the Dog, and of his friend Marilyn,* based on the book of the same name by Andrew O'Hagan, whose story follows Monroe's last two years, seen from the perspective of her pet dog, a gift from Frank Sinatra in 1960. George Clooney would play Sinatra. Despite everything, there has been no further response as to whether the production will go ahead.

2011-present: Professional expansion

In 2011, she made her debut as a film director in *In the Land of Blood and Honey* (2011), a love story between a Serbian soldier and a Bosnian prisoner during the Bosnian War (1992-95). She directed the film in order to revive attention to the survivors, after having visited Bosnia and Herzegovina twice in her role as UNHCR Goodwill Ambassador. To ensure authenticity, the film featured only actors from the former Yugoslavia - including Goran Kostić and Zana Marjanović - and incorporated their wartime experiences into its script. After its release, it received mixed reviews. Todd McCarthy of *The Hollywood Reporter* wrote: "Jolie deserves significant credit for creating such a powerful and oppressive atmosphere and staging the horrific events so believably, even if it's those same forces that will make people not want to see what's on screen." The film was nominated for a Golden Globe for Best Foreign Language Film and Jolie was named an honorary citizen of Sarajevo for raising awareness of the war.

"I've always been attracted to war movies. I've always been moved by them, but until then I'd never wanted to direct one. I was going through a period where I was thinking a lot about my ten years traveling in these [war] situations and all the people I met who had been through conflicts and how their lives were affected."

- Jolie on her directorial debut.

She was considered for the roles of Meredith Vickers in the film *Prometheus*, Tiffany Maxwell in *Silver Linings Playbook* and Dr. Ryan Stone in *Gravity,* but Charlize Theron, Jennifer Lawrence and Sandra Bullock, respectively, ended up being chosen. After being away from the movies for three and a half years, she starred in *Maleficent* (2014), a *live-action* re-imagining of the animated *Sleeping Beauty* (1959). Critical reception was mixed, but the actress's performance in the titular role was praised. Sherri Linden of *The Hollywood Reporter* said that Jolie "is the heart and soul" of the film, "and exerts a magnetic and effortless power." In its opening weekend, *Maleficent* earned almost seventy million at the American box office and over a hundred million in other markets, marking Jolie's appeal to audiences of all ages in action and fantasy films. Ultimately, it grossed 757.8 million dollars worldwide, making it the fourth highest-grossing film of the year and the most profitable film of the actress's career.

Jolie completed her second directorial effort with *Unbroken* (2014), based on the biography of Louis Zamperini (1917-2014), a former Olympic athlete who survived a plane crash during the Second World War and spent two years as a prisoner of war in a Japanese war camp. The script for the film was written by the Coen brothers, and Jack O'Connell starred as Zamperini. Initially, there was a positive reception, so it was considered a likely Oscar contender for the Best Picture and Best Director categories; however, it later ended up receiving mixed reviews and few awards recognition, although it was named one of the best films of the year by the National Board of Review and the American Film Institute. *Variety*'s Justin Chang noted that the film is "impeccable craftsmanship with sobriety," but considered it "an extraordinary story told in dutiful, not exceptional, terms." Financially, *Unbroken* exceeded industry expectations in its opening weekend, eventually earning more than 163 million dollars worldwide.

Her next work as a filmmaker came in the marital drama *By the Sea* (2015), in which she starred with her then-husband Brad Pitt, marking their first collaboration since 2005's *Mr. & Mrs. Smith*. The film was a deeply personal project for Jolie, who was inspired by the life of her own mother. Critics, however, singled it out as a "vanity project," causing it to receive a generally poor reception. Despite starring two of Hollywood's leading actors, the film received only a limited release.

First They Killed My Father, an adaptation of the book of the same name by Loung Ung, premiered on Netflix at the end of 2016. As well as directing the film, Jolie co-wrote its screenplay with Ung, a human rights activist who survived Cambodia's Khmer Rouge regime. Describing her as a "skillful and sensitive filmmaker," *Newsday*'s Rafer Guzmán praised her for "convincingly portraying [the] illogical hell of the Khmer Rouge era." The work was nominated for a Golden Globe and a BAFTA for Best Non-English Language Film.

Jolie reprised the role of Maleficent in *Mistress of Evil* (2019), which received unfavorable reviews from critics but grossed 490 million dollars. Her next work was *Come Away* (2020), an independent film directed by Brenda Chapman, which retold the stories of Alice in Wonderland

and Peter Pan. In 2021, he starred alongside Finn Little in the thriller *Those Who Wish Me Dead,* by director Taylor Sheridan, based on the book of the same name. Later that year, she made her debut in the Marvel Cinematic Universe, where she played Thena in Chloé Zhao's superhero film *Eternals.*

Her next work marks her return to directing, in the adaptation of Alessandro Baricco's book *Without Blood.* The film features Salma Hayek in the lead role and has not yet been released.

In October 2022, Jolie was announced as director Pablo Larraín's choice to play the Greek-American soprano Maria Callas in the biopic entitled *Maria*. The film is scheduled for release in 2024.

She will also star alongside Halle Berry in the action thriller *Maude v Maude, as* a spy directed by Roseanne Liang.

Humanitarian work

UNHCR Ambassador

Jolie first witnessed the effects of a humanitarian crisis while filming *Lara Croft: Tomb Raider* (2001) in war-torn Cambodia, an experience that she said gave her a greater understanding of the world. When she finished filming the movie and returned home, she contacted the United Nations High Commissioner for Refugees (UNHCR) for information on problematic places internationally. To find out more about conditions in these areas, she began visiting refugee camps around the world. In February 2001, she made her first visit to a refugee camp, an eighteen-day mission to Sierra Leone and Tanzania. She later expressed her shock at what she had witnessed. In the following months, Jolie returned to Cambodia for two weeks and met with Afghan refugees in Pakistan, where she donated one million dollars in response to an international emergency appeal from the UNHCR, the largest donation ever received from an individual private initiative. She covered all the costs related to her missions and shared the same rudimentary working and living conditions as the UNHCR field people on all her visits. Jolie was appointed Goodwill Ambassador at UNHCR headquarters in Geneva on August 27, 2001.

Over the next decade, he took part in more than forty field missions, meeting refugees and internally displaced people in more than thirty countries. In 2002, when asked what he hoped to achieve, he declared: "Raising awareness of the situation of these people, I think they should be praised for what they have survived, not despised." To this end, her 2001-02 field visits were chronicled in her book *Notes from My Travels*, published in October 2003 alongside the release of her film *Beyond Borders*. Jolie intended to visit what she called "forgotten emergencies," crises that had lost media attention. She distinguished herself by traveling to war zones, such as the Sudanese region of Darfur during the Darfur conflict, the Syrian-Iraqi border during the Second Gulf War, where she met privately with American troops and other multinational forces, and the Afghan capital, Kabul, during the Afghan War, where three aid workers were murdered during her first visit. To help her travel, she began taking flying lessons in 2004 with the aim of transporting aid workers and food supplies around the world; she now holds a private pilot's license with an instrument rating and owns a Cirrus SR22 and a single-engine Cessna 208 Caravan.

On April 17, 2012, after more than a decade of service as a UNHCR Goodwill Ambassador, Jolie was promoted to the position of Special Envoy to High Commissioner António Guterres, the first person to assume this position within the organization. In her new position, she was given the authority to represent Guterres and UNHCR on a diplomatic level, with a focus on major refugee crises. In the months following his promotion, he made his first visit as Special Envoy - the third person to do so - to Ecuador, where he met with Colombian refugees and accompanied Guterres on a week-long tour of Jordan, Lebanon, Turkey, and Iraq, to assess the situation of refugees from Syria. Since then, he has carried out more than a dozen field missions around the world.

Environmental conservation and community development

In an effort to connect her Cambodian-born son to his origins, Jolie bought a house in the country in 2003. The house is located on a 39-hectare property in the northwestern province of Battambang, next to Samlout National Park in the Cardamom Mountains. She bought sixty thousand hectares of the park and turned the area into a wildlife reserve in honor of her son, the Maddox Jolie Project. In recognition of her environmental conservation efforts, King Norodom Sihamoni granted her Cambodian citizenship on July 31, 2005.

In November 2006, Jolie expanded the project - renaming it the Maddox Jolie-Pitt Foundation (MJP) - to create Asia's first Millennium Village, in line with the UN's development goals. She was inspired by a meeting with the founder of the Millennium Promise, the noted economist Jeffrey Sachs, at the World Economic Forum in Davos, where she was a guest speaker in 2005 and 2006. In mid-2007, around 6,000 villagers and 72 employees - some of them former poachers - lived and worked at the MJP. The complex includes schools, roads and a soy milk factory, all financed by Jolie. Her house serves as the headquarters of the MJP camp. After filming *Beyond Borders* (2003) in Namibia, she became patron of the Harnas Wildlife Foundation, a wildlife orphanage and medical center in the Kalahari Desert. In December 2010, Jolie and her partner, Brad Pitt, founded the Shiloh Jolie-Pitt Foundation to support the conservation work of the Naankuse Wildlife Sanctuary, a nature reserve also located in the Kalahari. On behalf of their Namibian-born daughter, they have funded large animal conservation projects, as well as a free health clinic, housing and a school for the San Bushmen community in Naankuse. They both support other causes through the Jolie-Pitt Foundation, set up in September 2006.

Child immigration and education

Jolie has turned her attention to causes aimed at helping immigrant and other vulnerable children, both in the United States and in developing countries, including the "Unaccompanied Alien Child Protection Act of 2005". She began lobbying for humanitarian interests in the

American capital from 2003, explaining: "As much as I wish I didn't have to visit Washington, it's the only way to promote the cause." Since October 2008, she has co-chaired Kids in Need of Defense (KIND), a network of American law firms that provide free legal assistance to unaccompanied minors in immigration proceedings to the United States. Founded in collaboration between Jolie and the Microsoft Corporation, by 2013 KIND had become the main provider of *pro bono* lawyers for immigrant children. Jolie had previously, from 2005 to 2007, funded the launch of a similar initiative, and subsequently the U.S. Committee for Refugees and Immigrants launched the National Center for Refugee and Immigrant Children.

She also advocates for children's education. Since the founding of the Clinton Global Initiative's annual meeting in September 2007, she has co-chaired the Educational Partnership for Children of Conflict (EPCC), which provides funding for education programs for children in conflict-affected regions. In its first year, the partnership supported education projects for Iraqi refugee children, young people affected by the conflict in Darfur and girls in rural Afghanistan, among other conflict-affected groups. The partnership has worked closely with the Council on Foreign Relations' Center for Universal Education - founded by economist Gene Sperling - which aims to establish education policies, including making recommendations to UN agencies and the development agencies of the G8 and the World Bank. Since April 2013, all profits from Jolie's "high-end Jolie" and "Style of Jolie" jewelry collections have benefited the work of the partnership.

Jolie funded a school and boarding school for girls in the Kakuma refugee camp in northwestern Kenya, which opened in 2005, and two elementary school for girls in the Tangi and Qalai Gudar returnee settlements in eastern Afghanistan, which opened in March 2010 and November 2012 respectively. In addition to the *Millennium Village* facilities in Cambodia, the activist had already built at least ten other schools in the country by 2005. In February 2006, she opened the Maddox Chivan Children's Center, a medical and educational center that assists children affected by HIV, in the Cambodian capital, Phnom Penh. In Sebeta, Ethiopia, the birthplace of her eldest daughter, she funds the Zahara Children's Center, which opened in 2015 and aims to educate children suffering from HIV or tuberculosis. Both centers are run by the Global Health Committee.

Jolie has expressed her support for Malala Yousafzai, an activist for women's human rights and access to education for teenagers in Pakistan, known for having been shot by members of the Taliban after blogging for the BBC in Urdu about what life was like for people under the Taliban regime. After Yousafzai's shooting on October

9, 2012, Jolie wrote an article for *The Daily Beast* entitled "We All Are Malala", in which she documented her reaction to the event and expressed her support for girls' education in Pakistan. The following year, she gave a speech at the World Summit of Women, in which she expressed her support for Yousafzai and announced the start of the Malala Fund, a system of grants designed to support students in Pakistan. In addition, she personally contributed more than two hundred thousand dollars to the Fund and also honored Yousafzai by opening a school for girls in Pakistan.

Human rights and women's rights

After joining the Council on Foreign Relations (CFR) in June 2007, Jolie organized a conference on international law and justice at CFR headquarters and funded several special reports, including the "Intervention to Stop Genocide and Mass Atrocities." In January 2011, she established the Jolie Legal Fellowship, a network of lawyers who are sponsored to defend the continuity of human rights in their home countries. Its member lawyers, called *Jolie Legal Fellows*, have facilitated child protection efforts in Haiti after the 2010 earthquake and promoted the development of an inclusive democratic process in Libya after the 2011 revolution.

She supported a campaign by the British government on global action against sexual violence in military conflict zones, which made the issue a priority during the 2013 G8 meeting. In May 2012, she launched the Preventing Sexual Violence Initiative (PSVI) with the then British Foreign Secretary William Hague, who was inspired to campaign on the issue after watching *In the Land of Blood and Honey* (2011), a film directed by Jolie. PSVI was created to complement the work of the British government by raising awareness and promoting international cooperation. Jolie spoke about the issue at the G8 Foreign Ministers' meeting, where the nations present adopted a historic declaration before the UN Security Council: the G8 Chancellors agreed to make a call for increased efforts to seek justice for victims of abuse, including 35.5 million dollars in funding for prevention and response efforts. In June 2014, she co-chaired the International Summit to End Sexual Violence in Conflict, the largest meeting ever held on the subject, which resulted in a protocol approved by 151 nations.

Through her work at PSVI, Jolie met Arminka Helic, Hague's special adviser at the time. They founded Jolie Pitt Dalton Helic in 2015, dedicated to women's rights and international justice, among other causes. In May of the following year, she made her debut as a guest lecturer at the London School of Economics, sharing her experience of combating sexual violence with postgraduates on the Women, Peace and Security course.

In February 2017, the actress criticized, in an opinion piece published by *The New York Times, the* executive order signed by President Donald Trump suspending the United States Refugee Admissions Program (USRAP) for 120 days, as well as the entry of people from Libya, Iran, Iraq, Somalia, Sudan, Syria and Yemen.

Recognition and honors

Jolie has received widespread recognition for her humanitarian work. In August 2002, she received the Inaugural Humanitarian Award from the Immigration and Refugee Program of Church World Service and, in October of the following year, she was the first person to receive the Citizen of the World Award from the United Nations Correspondents' Association. She was awarded the Global Humanitarian Award by UNA-USA in October 2005 and received the Freedom Award from the International Rescue Committee in November 2007. In October 2011, the United Nations High Commissioner for Refugees, António Guterres, awarded her with a gold pin - reserved for senior members - in recognition of her being a UNHCR Goodwill Ambassador for over a decade.

In November 2013, Jolie was awarded the Jean Hersholt Humanitarian Award, an honorary Academy Award, by the Board of Governors of the Academy of Motion Picture Arts and Sciences. In June 2014, she was made an Honorary Commander of the Order of St Michael and St George (DCMG) for her services to UK foreign policy and the campaign to end sexual violence in war zones. In a private ceremony in October of the same year, the actress was made an Honorary Dame by Queen Elizabeth II and received an insignia at Buckingham Palace for her humanitarian work.

Because of her humanitarian efforts, she has been compared to Audrey Hepburn; she said: "I feel lucky and privileged to be able to be involved in this. And I'm sure Audrey does too. [...] She was able to help millions of children around the world. There have been refugees in need of help for a long time. And I'm sure, you know, that my children will visit and learn from refugees in the future."

Personal life

Relationships and marriages

Jolie began a serious relationship at the age of fourteen, which lasted two years. Her mother allowed her to live with her boyfriend in their home, about which she later said: "Either I would be reckless on the streets with my boyfriend or he would be with me in my room, with my mother in the next room. She made the choice and, because of that, I continued to go to school every morning and explored my first relationship in a safe way." She compared the relationship to a marriage in its emotional intensity, and said that the break-up forced her to dedicate herself to her acting career at the age of sixteen.

During the filming of *Hackers* (1995), she began an affair with British actor Jonny Lee Miller, her first boyfriend since their teenage relationship. They didn't keep in touch for many months after the production ended, but they met again and got married in March 1996. She attended her wedding in black rubber pants and a white T-shirt, on which she had written her fiancé's name in her own blood. Although the marriage ended the following year, Jolie remained on good terms with Miller, whom she called "a solid man and friend." Her divorce, which she initiated in February 1999, was finalized shortly before she remarried the following year.

Shortly before meeting and marrying Miller, Jolie had a romantic relationship with model Jenny Shimizu during the filming of *Foxfire* (1996). She later said: "I probably would have married Jenny if I hadn't married my husband. I fell in love with her the first second I saw her." According to Shimizu, the relationship lasted several years and continued even while Jolie was romantically involved with other people.

"Of course, if I fell in love with a woman tomorrow, and I felt it was okay to want to kiss her and touch her. If I fell in love with her? Absolutely! Yes!"

- Jolie when talking about her bisexuality.

After dating actor Billy Bob Thornton for two months, they got married in Las Vegas on May 5, 2000. They met while filming *Pushing Tin* (1999), but didn't pursue a relationship at the time, as Thornton was involved with actress Laura Dern, while Jolie reportedly dated actor Timothy Hutton, her castmate in *Playing God* (1997). As a result of their frequent public declarations of passion and gestures of love - most famously, both wearing vials of each other's blood around their necks - their marriage became a favorite topic of the entertainment media. Jolie and Thornton announced the adoption of a child from

Cambodia in March 2002, but suddenly separated three months later; their divorce was finalized on May 27, 2003. When asked about the sudden end of her marriage, she said: "It took me by surprise too, because from one day to the next we changed completely. And it's scary, but ... I think it can happen when you get involved [with someone] and you don't know yourself yet."

Jolie became involved in a scandal that attracted a lot of press attention when she was accused of causing the divorce of actors Brad Pitt and Jennifer Aniston in 2005. She had fallen in love with Pitt during the filming of *Mr. & Mrs. Smith* (2005), but denied the accusations of an affair, saying: "Being intimate with a married man, when my own father cheated on my mother, is not something I can forgive, I couldn't look at myself in the morning if I did that, I wouldn't be attracted to a man who would cheat on his wife." Jolie and Pitt didn't comment publicly on their relationship until January 2006, when she confirmed that she was pregnant with his child.

During their twelve-year relationship, "Brangelina" - an acronym created by the media - was the subject of worldwide media coverage. After the initial scandal subsided, they became one of Hollywood's most glamorous couples. Their family grew to six children, three of whom were adopted, before they announced their engagement in April 2012. They married on August

23, 2014, at their Château Miraval estate in Correns, France. She subsequently took the surname Jolie Pitt. After two years of marriage, the couple separated in September 2016, declaring irreconcilable differences; in her divorce petition, Jolie asked for custody of their children.

Children

On March 10, 2002, Jolie adopted her first child, seven-month-old Maddox Chivan, at an orphanage in Battambang, Cambodia, who before his adoption was called Rath Vibol, born on August 5, 2001, in a local village. After visiting the country twice, while filming *Lara Croft: Tomb Raider* (2001) and on a UNHCR field mission, she returned in November 2001 with her then husband, Billy Bob Thornton, where she met Maddox and subsequently applied to adopt him. The adoption process was halted the following month when the US government banned adoptions in Cambodia because of allegations of child trafficking. Although Jolie's adoption facilitator was later convicted of visa fraud and money laundering, the child's adoption was deemed legal. After the process was finalized, she took custody of him in Namibia, where she was filming *Beyond Borders* (2003). The couple announced the joint adoption, but she adopted Maddox and raised him alone after their separation three months later.

In July 2005, Jolie adopted a six-month-old girl called Zahara Marley from an orphanage in Addis Ababa, Ethiopia. Zahara, formerly Yemsrach, was born on January 8, 2005, in Awasa, Ethiopia. Jolie initially believed that Zahara was an AIDS-positive orphan, as her grandmother had told a testimony, but her mother subsequently denied the testimony and explained that she had abandoned her family when Zahara became ill and said that she considered her "very happy" to have been adopted by the actress. When she traveled to Ethiopia to take custody of Zahara, she was accompanied by her ex-partner Brad Pitt. She later said that they had made the decision to adopt in Ethiopia together, having visited the country at the beginning of the year. After Jolie announced her intention to adopt her children, she filed a petition to legally change her surname from Jolie to Jolie-Pitt, which was granted on January 19, 2006. Angelina then adopted Maddox and Zahara shortly afterwards.

In order to avoid the inevitable unprecedented media uproar surrounding their relationship, Jolie and Pitt traveled to Namibia for the birth of their first biological daughter. On May 27, 2006, she gave birth to a daughter, Shiloh Nouvel, in Swakopmund. The couple sold the first photos of the child through the Getty Images image bank with the aim of benefiting charitable organizations, rather than allowing *paparazzi to* take the pictures. *People* and *Hello!* magazines bought the American and British rights to the images for 4.1 and 3.5 million dollars respectively, a record in celebrity photojournalism at the time, and all proceeds were donated to UNICEF. The girl always appeared in public dressed in men's clothes and haircuts and never hid her desire to be a boy. A wish fully supported by her family. In 2020, it was announced in the press that Shiloh, at the age of 14, had started gender reassignment treatments, but at the end of 2021, Shiloh grew her hair out and started wearing more feminine clothes, such as dresses.

In March 2007, Jolie adopted a three-year-old son, Pax Thien, from an orphanage in Ho Chi Minh, Vietnam. Formerly known as Pham Quang Sang, the boy was born on November 29, 2003, and had been abandoned by his biological mother shortly after his birth. After visiting the orphanage with Pitt in November 2006, Jolie applied for adoption as a single mother, because the country's adoption regulations do not allow unmarried couples to adopt children. After her return to the United States, she asked the court to change her son's surname from Jolie to Jolie-Pitt, which was approved on May 31. Pitt subsequently adopted Pax on February 21, 2008.

At the Cannes Film Festival in May 2008, Jolie confirmed that she was expecting twins. During the two weeks she spent in a seaside hospital in Nice, France, reporters and photographers camped out there during her stay. She gave birth to a boy, Knox Léon, and a girl, Vivienne Marcheline, on July 12, 2008. The first photos of the children were sold jointly to *People* and *Hello!* for fourteen million dollars - the most expensive celebrity photographs ever bought. All profits were donated to the Jolie-Pitt Foundation.

Cancer prevention treatment

On February 16, 2013, at the age of 37, the actress underwent a preventive double mastectomy after learning that she had an 87% risk of developing breast cancer due to a defective BRCA1 gene. Her maternal family history justified the BRCA mutations: her mother had breast cancer and died of ovarian cancer, while her grandmother died of ovarian cancer; her aunt, who had the same BRCA1 defect, died of breast cancer three months after Jolie's operation. After the mastectomy, which reduced her chances of developing breast cancer to less than five percent, the actress underwent reconstructive surgery involving implants and allografts. Two years later, in March 2015, following the results of tests that indicated possible signs of early ovarian cancer, she underwent a preventive oophorectomy, as she had a 50% risk of developing the cancer due to the same genetic anomaly. Despite hormone replacement therapy, the surgery brought on her premature menopause.

After completing the operations, she discussed the precedents in *op-eds* for *The New York Times, with the* aim of helping other women make informed health-related choices. She detailed her diagnosis, surgeries and personal experiences, and described her decision to undergo preventive surgery as a proactive measure for the sake of her six children. She also wrote: "On a personal note, I don't feel less of a woman. I made a strong choice that in no way diminishes my femininity."

Her announcement about her mastectomy attracted press attention, as well as new discussions about BRCA mutations and genetic testing. Her decision was met with praise from several public figures, while health promoters supported her awareness of the options available to women at risk. Dubbed *The Angelina Effect in Time's* cover article, Jolie's influence has led to a "global and lasting" increase in BRCA genetic testing: testing has increased twofold in Australia and the United Kingdom, parts of Canada and India, as well as increasing significantly in other European countries and the United States. Researchers in Canada and the UK found that, despite the huge increase [in testing], the percentage of carriers of the mutation remained the same, meaning that Jolie's message had only reached those most at risk.

In the media

Public image

As the daughter of actor Jon Voight, Jolie appeared in the media from an early age. After starting her own career, she gained a reputation as a "wild child," and this contributed to her early success in the late 1990s and early 2000s. The media often reported on her fascination with blood and knives, experiments with drugs and her sex life, particularly her bisexuality and interest in sadomasochism. In 2000, when asked about her outspokenness, she stated: "I say things that other people can go through, that's what artists should do - get things off their chest and not be perfect and not have answers for anything, and see if people understand." Another factor that contributed to her controversial image were tabloid rumors of incest that began when, upon winning her Oscar, she kissed her brother on the lips and said: "I'm so in love with my brother right now." She refuted the rumors, saying: "It was disappointing that something so beautiful and pure could be turned into a circus," and explained that, as children of divorce, she and James trust each other.

Jolie's reputation began to change positively after, at the age of 26, she became a Goodwill Ambassador for the

United Nations High Commissioner for Refugees; about this, she commented: "In my twenties, I was fighting with myself. Now, I'm fighting for something important." Due to his extensive activism, his *Q Score* more than doubled between 2000 and 2006. His popularity grew progressively; in 2006, he was familiar to 81% of Americans, compared to 31% in 2000; in 2020, that figure jumped to 96%. He became notable for his ability to positively influence his public image through his achievements, without employing a publicity agent. Her *Q Score* remained above average even when, in 2005, she was accused of breaking up Brad Pitt's marriage to Jennifer Aniston, at which point her public persona became an unlikely combination of alleged mistress, mother, sex symbol and humanitarian. A decade later, she was considered the most admired woman in the world in global surveys conducted by YouGov in 2015, 2016 and 2018 and was ranked second in 2019. In 2014, YouGov published that the actress was named the most influential famous person when it comes to political issues.

Jolie's general influence and wealth are widely reported. In a 2006 global survey carried out by ACNielsen in 42 international markets, the actress, along with Pitt, was considered the favorite celebrity to endorse brands and products worldwide. She was the face of St. John and Shiseido from 2006 to 2008, and in 2011 had a deal with Louis Vuitton worth ten million dollars - a record for a single advertising campaign. Jolie was in the Time *100*, a list of the most influential people in the world published by *Time* magazine, in 2006 and 2008. She was named the world's most powerful celebrity in the 2009 edition of *Forbes,* and was listed as the most powerful actress from 2006 to 2008 and from 2011 to 2013. The magazine also cited her as Hollywood's highest paid actress in 2009, 2011 and 2013, with estimated annual earnings of 27 million, 30 million and 33 million dollars respectively.

Appearance

Jolie's public image is strongly linked to her beauty and sex appeal. Many media outlets, including *Vogue*, *People* and *Vanity Fair, have* ranked her as the most beautiful woman in the world, while others such as *Esquire*, *FHM* and *Empire* have named her the sexiest woman alive. Both titles have often been based on public polls in which Jolie has come out far ahead of other celebrities. Her best-known physical features are her tattoos, her eyes and, in particular, her pouty lips; the *New York Times* considered her chin to be like Kirk Douglas and her eyes like Bette Davis. Among her twenty or so tattoos are the Latin proverb *quod me nutrit me destruit* (in Portuguese: "what nourishes me destroys me"), the Tennessee Williams quote "A prayer to the wild-hearted kept in cages," four Sanskrit Buddhist prayers of protection, a twelve-inch tiger and geographical coordinates indicating the places where she met her adopted children. Over time, she has covered or had laser surgery on several of her tattoos, including "Billy Bob", the name of her second husband. Her photo with blood dripping from her mouth was the inspiration for the posters for the movie *Jennifer's Body* and the series *True Blood*. The photograph was taken in 2003 by Martin Schoeller and is part of his *close-up* collection. In November 2016, the image was put up for sale for sixty thousand dollars - something like 190,000 reais at the time.

In *FHM*'s publication of the world's Hundred Sexiest Women, Jolie was ranked 61st in 2001, 32nd in 2003, ninth in 2004, third in 2005, fourth in 2006, eighth in 2007, ninth in 2008, 14th in 2009, 70th in 2010, 90th in 2011, 31st in 2012, and 72nd in 2015. In 2011, *Men's Health* placed her tenth on a list of the hundred most attractive women of all time. She also appeared on *Maxim* magazine's *Hot* 100 list at number 43 in 2003, seventeen in 2004, seven in 2005, four in 2006, twelve in 2007, 26 in 2009, 38 in 2010. She was considered one of the fifty most beautiful people in the world by *People magazine in* 1998, 2004 and 2005, and was voted number one out of the hundred people in the magazine's magazine of the same content in 2006; she was included in the 2007, 2008 and 2009 editions, and was also classified as one of the 25 most intriguing people in 2010, 2013 and 2014. The actress came second in the *Hot* 100 list of the *online* LGBT portal AfterEllen.com in 2007. She repeated her appearance in the following years, being voted eleventh on the list in 2008, ninth in 2009 and thirteenth in 2010.

Empire magazine ranked her second in its list of the "100 Sexiest Movie Stars Ever" in 2004, she was included again in the publication in 2007, being voted number one, and in the 2013 edition she came in at number nine. *Esquire* ran a publication in 2007 with the same title, and the actress also topped the list. In 2000, she was named by *USA Today* as number one in the publication of the hundred people of the year, number thirty-three in 2001, sixty-one in 2002, sixty-eight in 2003, and number three in 2005.

Professionally, the actress's *status* as a sex symbol was seen as both an asset and an obstacle. Some of her most commercially successful films, including *Lara Croft: Tomb Raider* (2001) and *Beowulf* (2007), openly relied, at least in part, on her sex appeal, with *Empire* claiming that her "curvaceous figure," "alluring eyes" and "lips" greatly contributed to her appeal to movie audiences. On the other hand, *Salon* writer Allen Barra agreed with critics who suggested that Jolie's "dark, intense sexuality" limited her in terms of the types of roles she could play, while Clint Eastwood, who directed *Changeling* (2008), opined that "having the most beautiful face on the planet" sometimes undermined her dramatic credibility with audiences.

In addition to her career, Jolie's appearance is credited with having influenced popular culture in general. In 2002, Sarah Warn, founder of *AfterEllen,* noted that many women of different sexual orientations have publicly expressed attraction to Jolie, which Warn called "a new development in American culture," adding that "there are many beautiful women in Hollywood and few generate the same kind of colossal interest in [different] genders and sexual orientations as she does." Jolie's physical attributes have become highly sought after among Western women seeking cosmetic surgery. In 2007, she was considered "the gold standard of beauty," and her plump lips were the most imitated feature of the actress in the 2010s. *Superdrug* named her "the beauty icon of the 2000s"; Steve Jebson, commercial director of *Superdrug*, said: "Angelina Jolie is not a conventional beauty, but her strong character shines through her fabulous features to give her a unique position in the beauty world." After a 2011 survey by *Allure*, it was discovered that she more than represented the American beauty ideal, compared to model Christie Brinkley in 1991, having "branched out beyond the Barbie doll ideal and embraced something very different." In 2013, *Time*'s Jeffrey Kluger agreed that Jolie symbolized the feminine ideal for many years and opined that her frank discussion of her double mastectomy redefined her beauty.

Filmography

Over the course of her career, Jolie has appeared in a number of films and telefilms, receiving critical acclaim for her performances, particularly in *George Wallace* (1997), *Gia* (1998), *Girl, Interrupted* (1999), which won her a Golden Globe and an Oscar for Best Supporting Actress, *A Mighty Heart (*2007), *Wanted* and *Changeling* (both 2008), which earned her an Oscar nomination for Best Actress, and *Maleficent (*2014). Her most profitable films are: *Maleficent*, the *Kung Fu Panda* trilogy, *Mr. & Mrs. Smith (*2005), *Shark Tale (*2004), *Wanted, Salt* and *The Tourist (*both 2010), *Lara Croft: Tomb Raider* (2001) and *Gone in 60 Seconds (*2000).

Awards and nominations

Throughout her career, Jolie has won and been nominated for numerous awards, notably her Oscar nominations for Best Actress, Golden Globe nominations for Best Actress in a Motion Picture Drama for two consecutive years (2007 and 2008), Best Actress in a Comedy or Musical and Best Foreign Language Film (as producer), four BAFTA, Emmy for Best Actress in a Miniseries or Telefilm and Best Supporting Actress in a Miniseries or Telefilm and the Screen Actors Guild for Best Leading Actress in a Motion Picture in 2008 and

2009. She won the Oscar for Best Supporting Actress in 2000, the Golden Globe for three consecutive years (1998, 1999 and 2000), two Screen Actors Guild awards in 1999 and 2000.

As a humanitarian, she won the Jean Hersholt Humanitarian Award in 2013 and other awards, including the Order of St. Michael and St. George and the United Nations Correspondents' Association. By 2017, Jolie had been nominated for 97 different awards, winning 49 of them.

Other books by United Library

https://campsite.bio/unitedlibrary

Milton Keynes UK
Ingram Content Group UK Ltd.
UKHW020654040324
438885UK00018B/1060

9 789464 902075